A Note from
Mary Pope Osborne

MAGIC TREE HOUSE®

FACT TRACKERS

When I write Magic Tree House® adventures,
I love including facts about the times and
places Jack and Annie visit. But when readers
finish these adventures, I want them to learn
even more. So that's why we write a series of
nonfiction books that are companions to the
fiction titles in the Magic Tree House® series. We
call these books Fact Trackers because we love
to track the facts! Whether we're researching
dinosaurs, pyramids, Pilgrims, sea monsters, or
cobras, we're always amazed at how wondrous
and surprising the real world is. We want you
to experience the same wonder we do—so get
out your pencils and notebooks and hit the trail
with us. You can be a Magic Tree House® Fact
Tracker, too!

Mary Pope Osborne

Here's what kids, parents, and teachers have to say about the Magic Tree House® Fact Trackers:

"They are so good. I can't wait for the next one. All I can say for now is prepare to be amazed!" —Alexander N.

"I have read every Magic Tree House book there is. The [Fact Trackers] are a thrilling way to get more information about the special events in the story." —John R.

"These are fascinating nonfiction books that enhance the magical time-traveling adventures of Jack and Annie. I love these books, especially *American Revolution*. I was learning so much, and I didn't even know it!" —Tori Beth S.

"[They] are an excellent 'behind-the-scenes' look at what the [Magic Tree House fiction] has started in your imagination! You can't buy one without the other; they are such a complement to one another." —Erika N., mom

"Magic Tree House [Fact Trackers] took my children on a journey from Frog Creek, Pennsylvania, to so many significant historical events! The detailed manuals are a remarkable addition to the classic fiction Magic Tree House books we adore!" —Jenny S., mom

"[They] are very useful tools in my classroom, as they allow for students to be part of the planning process. Together, we find facts in the [Fact Trackers] to extend the learning introduced in the fictional companions. Researching and planning classroom activities, such as our class Olympics based on facts found in *Ancient Greece and the Olympics*, help create a genuine love for learning!" —Paula H., teacher

Magic Tree House®
Fact Tracker

DRAGONS AND MYTHICAL CREATURES

A nonfiction companion to
Magic Tree House® #55:
Night of the Ninth Dragon

by Mary Pope Osborne
and Natalie Pope Boyce

illustrated by Carlo Molinari

A STEPPING STONE BOOK™
Random House New York

Visit us on the Web!
SteppingStonesBooks.com
MagicTreeHouse.com

Educators and librarians, for a variety of teaching tools, visit us at
RHTeachersLibrarians.com

Library of Congress Cataloging-in-Publication Data
Osborne, Mary Pope, author. Boyce, Natalie Pope, author.
Dragons and mythical creatures / by Mary Pope Osborne and Natalie Pope
Boyce ; illustrated by Carlo Molinari.
Description: New York : Random House, [2015]
Series: Magic tree house fact tracker
"A nonfiction companion to Magic tree house #55: Night of the Ninth Dragon."
LCCN 2015027169 ISBN 978-1-101-93636-8 (trade) —
ISBN 978-1-101-93637-5 (lib. bdg.) — ISBN 978-1-101-93638-2 (ebook)
1. Dragons—Juvenile literature. 2. Animals, Mythical—Juvenile literature.
LCC GR830.D7 O78 2015 DDC 398.24/54—dc23

Printed in the United States of America

10 9 8 7 6 5 4 3 2 1

This book has been officially leveled by using the F&P Text Level Gradient™
Leveling System.

For Phoebe Landolf, a magical kid!

Historical Consultant:

ROBERT LONGSWORTH, Emeritus Professor of English, Oberlin College

Education Consultant:

HEIDI JOHNSON, language acquisition and science education specialist, Bisbee, Arizona

Special thanks to our loyal Random House team: Mallory Loehr, Paula Sadler, Jenna Lettice, Heather Palisi, Carlo Molinari for his great illustrations, and as always, to our skillful, ever-patient editor, Diane Landolf

DRAGONS AND MYTHICAL CREATURES

Contents

Dear Readers,

In <u>Night of the Ninth Dragon</u>, we traveled with King Arthur and Queen Guinevere to the legendary Isle of Avalon. During our adventures, we met incredible mythical animals like dragons, unicorns, and mermaids. When we got home, we wondered about these amazing creatures.

We did a lot of research, and to our surprise we discovered that hundreds of years ago, people actually believed dragons and other mythical animals lived in their forests, seas, and skies! They often made up stories about them to explain things in nature they didn't understand—like lightning, thunder, and how the world began.

For thousands of years, people all over the world told rich tales of mythical beasts.

Ancient Greeks, Romans, Chinese, and many other countries and cultures had legends and myths of dragons who were either very good or very deadly. There were tales of beautiful mermaids whose songs caused sailors to wreck their ships. There were stories of great sea monsters that look a lot like giant squids and dragged ships to the bottom of the sea.

What we found was so exciting, we just had to share it with you. So grab your notebooks, and let's go explore the strange and mysterious world of mythical beasts!

Jack
Annie

1

Dragons and Other Mythical Creatures

If you lived thousands of years ago, you probably wouldn't know how to read. Most people didn't. There were almost no books or schools. And no homework, either!

Since no one had telephones, computers, or even newspapers, all the news you'd ever hear came from other people.

You probably wouldn't ever have traveled too far from home. If you did, you walked or got on a boat or found a horse to take you.

No one knew much about science. It was hard to answer questions like why the sun went down at night or what caused thunderstorms, eclipses, rain, and wind.

 An eclipse can be scary if you don't know what's happening. It looks like the sun or moon is disappearing!

People knew about the wild animals that lived near them, but not in other parts of the world.

In order to explain these mysteries, people created stories called *myths*. Myths are often about gods, goddesses, and heroes with amazing powers. Many stories also have *mythical* animals. As the years passed, many people came to believe that these creatures were real.

Mythical comes from the word <u>myth</u> and means imaginary and not real.

For example, many native people of North America had stories about a great bird called the Thunderbird. When the Thunderbird flapped its enormous wings, thunder shook the earth! When the bird blinked its flashing eyes, lightning ripped across the sky.

In Vietnam, people thought a giant

Vietnamese mossy toad

toad or frog caused eclipses. It gobbled up the sun and moon!

Stories to Entertain

Stories weren't just for explaining nature. Storytelling was also fun. It was a great way to get through a long winter's night. Kids and adults gathered around to listen to exciting tales of mythical heroes who fought animals with amazing powers.

16

Parents told myths and other stories to their children. Their children told the same stories to *their* children.

Years later, people started writing down these exciting tales. Today most bookstores and libraries have books about mythical animals from all over the world.

Many of the stories about dragons, unicorns, mermaids, and others are the same ones that children listened to long ago.

Explorers and Writers

Ideas about mythical creatures also came from explorers who had been to faraway lands. When they returned, they talked about the animals they'd seen.

People used their imaginations to picture them. And sometimes the pictures in their head were really wild!

Writers described animals that they

had only heard of but never seen. They thought that what they wrote was true.

Pliny the Elder

Pliny the *Elder* was a famous Roman writer. He lived from AD 23 to 79.

Pliny wrote a book called *Natural History*. He meant it to be about science, not about myths and make-believe.

Pliny thought that dragons and unicorns were real. He said some surprising things about them.

Pliny wrote that dragons wrapped themselves around elephants and tied

Elder means older. Pliny had an adopted son who was also a writer. He was Pliny the Younger.

them up in knots. He also said that even though the elephants untied the knots with their trunks, the dragons killed them anyway . . . and drank all their blood! Yikes! (NOT TRUE!)

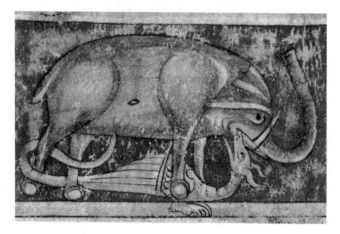

The Middle Ages are also called medievial times.

Bestiaries

The Middle Ages in Europe began about 1,500 years ago and ended about 500 years ago. This was the time of kings, queens, knights, and castles.

A popular kind of book then was a *bestiary*. This is a book full of pictures and descriptions of animals.

Bestiaries were often written by Christian monks. Because there were no printing presses, each book had to be copied by hand.

The word **bestiary** comes from the Latin word **bestia**, which means **beast**.

The colorful pictures in bestiaries helped people who couldn't read.

Many bestiaries had lessons about how to be a good Christian. The animals in them were symbols for good and evil.

 Some of the creatures, such as griffins, came from Greek myths.

Dragons and snakes were often symbols of the devil. Tigers, unicorns, and lions stood for healing and strength.

Animals in Art

During the Middle Ages, artists painted pictures of many different animals. Sometimes they painted them on walls or furniture. Some of the pictures are of real animals, like snakes, dogs, and sheep. Others show mythical creatures, such as unicorns, mermaids, griffins, and dragons.

Craftsmen carved these animals on stone churches and other buildings.

Weavers wove dragons, unicorns, and other beasts on beautiful tapestries. The most famous are a series of seven tapestries called *The Hunt of the Unicorn*. They tell the story of hunters chasing and killing a unicorn.

The Hunt of the Unicorn

A Unicorn's Horn for the Queen

In 1577, an English explorer named Martin Frobisher sailed to Canada. Frobisher and his crew found a large, dead fishlike animal stuck in ice. A long horn sprouted from its forehead. They thought it was a sea unicorn! Frobisher brought the horn back to England and gave it to Queen Elizabeth I.

The queen was so happy that she gave Frobisher 10,000 pounds. That was the price of a castle! The queen kept the horn locked away with her precious jewels.

The horn was really a narwhal's tusk. These rare whales live in the waters of the Arctic.

2

Dragons

What do you picture when you hear the word *dragon*? Is it a monster that breathes fire or a magical creature that brings good luck?

The answer might depend on where you live or what culture you come from. In stories from Europe, dragons are deadly winged reptiles that love to eat people for breakfast, lunch, and dinner. They are evil, greedy beasts.

Dragon myths began in China and other parts of Asia over 4,000 years ago.

The Chinese have a different view of dragons. In Chinese culture, dragons are the best and smartest of all animals. Even in modern China, dragons are honored as symbols of good luck and strength.

Dragon dance, Hong Kong

The Great Dragons of China

Two thousand years ago, a Chinese emperor named Qin Shihuangdi admired dragons. He honored them so much that he made his people call him the True Dragon, the Son of Heaven. His throne became the dragon throne, and his hands were dragon claws.

For years afterward, almost every emperor called himself the Dragon. The emperors wore special dragon robes with dragon patterns sewn on them. No one else was allowed to have dragons on their clothes.

People could even be put to death if they wore dragon robes!

Dragon robe

In the early Chinese empire, yellow dragons were the most royal. Later, red dragons took their place. Even today many people in China believe that red is a very lucky color.

Appearance

Pictures of Chinese dragons show large snakelike creatures covered in scales. Their faces often look like crocodiles' or other reptiles'.

Many have long chin whiskers and horns that look like deer antlers. Some have pearls tucked under their neck.

Pearls mean good luck in China.

Chinese dragons have four legs and feet with sharp claws. The emperors' dragons always have five claws on each foot, while other dragons have three or four.

In some Chinese stories, dragons can

change size. They can be so huge that they fill up the sky. Other times, they become small enough to fit in a teacup.

Habitat

Chinese dragons are mostly sea creatures. Some stories say that four main dragons rule seas to the north, south,

These sea dragons are part of the Nine-Dragon Wall in the Forbidden City, in Beijing, China.

east, and west of the country. The most powerful is the dragon of the Eastern Seas.

Dragons are said to spend winters in ocean palaces made of glittering jewels. Shrimp soldiers guard them, and crab generals command their armies.

Rising for the Rain

In spring, dragons rise into the sky, using magic bumps on their heads. As they soar out of the water, a huge clap of thunder shakes the heavens. Dark clouds gather, and rain beats down on the dry fields below.

Chinese stories tell of dragons that control weather and the seasons. Temples along the Chinese coast often have dragons carved on them. When floods came, people used to go to the temples to ask the dragons for help.

 This dragon sits on the roof of a Buddhist temple.

European Dragons

Many European dragon tales were based on Greek myths. Over the years, people added their own dragon stories.

During the Middle Ages, people imagined that dragons prowled the countryside at night looking for a midnight snack of people, cattle, or sheep.

Stinky Caves and Lairs

A medieval dragon's home is called its lair. Dragon lairs can be in riverbanks, caves, or the ruins of castles and other large buildings.

The bones of their victims are said to litter the floors.

A dragon's lair

European dragons are greedy. They love gold and precious stones. They fiercely guard their treasure and even sleep on top of it at night.

Appearance

Dragons of the Middle Ages look like lizards with long tails and scaly bodies.

 The explorer Marco Polo described dragons that looked like the ones in this painting.

Sharp, jagged ridges run down their backs. They have four wings that are similar to bat wings. Most of them breathe fire out of their mouths and noses. One blast of their fiery breath can kill. One twist of their powerful tail is enough to choke animals and people to death!

People believed that their breath was poisonous.

Dragon Tales

In the Middle Ages, stories about knights fighting dragons were very popular. Knights are the forces for good. Their brave deeds teach that good can defeat evil.

The most famous dragon story in Great Britain is about St. George. There are many different versions of the tale.

In one version, a fierce dragon was causing terror in the countryside. Every

St. George and the Dragon

day the dragon forced people to give it a sheep to eat.

When the sheep were gone, the dragon asked for young girls. After the dragon had killed all the other girls, it took the king's beautiful daughter. The king asked St. George for help right away.

St. George rode up to the dragon's cave. The poor princess stood there waiting to die. Suddenly a huge dragon charged out of the cave. Its roars shook the ground!

St. George tried to thrust a spear into the dragon, but its hard scales broke it.

Then St. George leapt from his horse and whipped out a sword. He struck the dragon under a wing where there were no scales. The mighty beast fell dead at his feet! For his reward, St. George got to marry the beautiful princess. Yay!

Two other legendary European dragon slayers were Siegfried and Beowulf.

The Red and the White Dragons

Merlin was a wise magician in the court of King Arthur in Camelot. When

Vortigern and the dragons

King Arthur's father was Uther Pendragon. **Pendragon** means Head Dragon.

Merlin was just a boy, he helped a Celtic king named Vortigern.

The king was trying to build a castle on a mountaintop. Every night something tore the castle down.

Merlin told the king that two dragons

lived in a lake under the mountain. Their nightly fights caved in the castle walls.

The king's men dug deep into the mountain. Two sleeping dragons, one red and one white, sprang up and began to fight. The white dragon escaped. The red one went back to sleep.

From then on, work on the castle went well. Ever since, a red dragon has been on the Welsh flag as a sign of strength and courage. The white dragon became a symbol for England.

welsh flag

Coats of Arms

Kings and knights had colorful shields and banners decorated with symbols that stood for their families. Each family had its own decoration, called a coat of arms. A coat of arms was a way to show family pride. Many displayed mythical creatures that had special meaning for the family.

When knights were on a battlefield, they found one another by looking for certain coats of arms. It was hard to see their faces under all that armor!

Some of the most popular symbols were:

Dragon: Defender of treasures

Lion: Courage

Elephant: Strength and courage

Fox: Intelligence

Wolf: Dangerous enemy

3

Sea Creatures

Oceans have their own secrets. Their dark waters hide many animals that live far under the sea. Even today 95 percent of the ocean is still unexplored. There could be millions of creatures we have not discovered yet.

Sailors long ago never knew what might be lurking under the waters. They heard stories of terrible sea creatures that attacked ships as they sailed peacefully on the sea. For example, Pliny the Elder wrote that thirty-foot-long monsters destroyed many of Alexander the Great's ships.

Creating a Sea Monster

For years, sailors returned home with tales of incredible sea serpents they'd seen on their voyages.

In the 1500s, an explorer named Sir Humphrey Gilbert sailed near Canada. On his way home, Sir Humphrey was shocked to see a beast with glaring eyes that looked like a lion! Sir Humphrey's imagination had created a sea monster.

When sailors saw animals like whales, squids, and octopuses, their fears ran wild. They dreamed up all sorts of weird and dangerous sea monsters.

What if a squid's tentacles were long enough to pull a ship to the bottom of the sea? Maybe there were whales as big as an island. Things could be very dangerous out there!

Mythical Maps

Sailors wanted to know where dangerous sea creatures lived. Early mapmakers tried to warn them by drawing pictures of mythical animals on their maps. The pictures marked places where sea monsters had been reported.

Olaus Magnus, a famous Swedish writer, also heard tales of sea monsters. He wrote a book about Swedish history. It said that sailors had spotted 200-foot-long sea serpents! They had flashing eyes and long, scraggly hair around their necks.

According to Olaus, they were covered with sharp black scales. He claimed

Even today people report sea serpent sightings.

47

that one sea serpent was so gigantic, it could coil around a ship's mast.

 In 1539, Olaus Magnus made a map called the Carta Marina that showed monsters he thought lived in the sea.

Kraken

One of the most well-known sea monsters is the kraken. Stories say that krakens live off the coasts of Norway and Iceland.

Krakens are gigantic. On the surface, they look like floating islands. Their arms are over a mile long. When they spread them out, they look like an island chain!

Some stories say that krakens look like giant crabs.

Pierre Denys de Montfort illustrated a kraken in his 1802 book on natural history.

The Bishop and the Kraken

In 1752, the bishop of Bergen, Norway, wrote a book called *The Natural History of Norway*. In it, he described a kraken sighting.

Sailors told him that when the kraken plunged down into the ocean, its huge body created a whirlpool. It was so powerful that it dragged a ship down into the sea. The bishop wrote that the kraken's arms could toss boats in the air like they were matchsticks!

Fishing with the Kraken

Other stories said that fish loved the smell of kraken. When krakens rested on the ocean floor, fish swarmed over their backs.

When a kraken surfaced, the fish tumbled off in a shimmering cascade. Long ago,

if fishermen had a good catch, people might
have asked if they'd been fishing on top of
a kraken!

Kappa

The Japanese tell stories of water spirits
called kappas. They live in lakes and rivers.

These little guys are the size of kids but
are much stronger than grown-ups. They

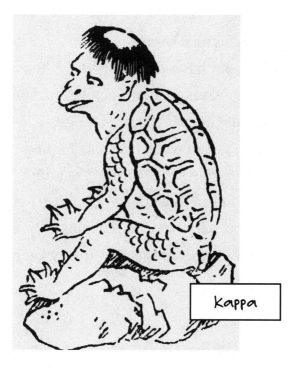

Kappa

Kappas also have beaks and webbed feet.

have monkey faces and arms and legs like frogs. Their bodies are covered with a shell like a turtle's.

Kappas can be helpful, but usually they are very tricky and dangerous. Their idea of fun is to pull people under the water and drown them. They also think it's fun to eat kids. But their favorite food of all is cucumbers!

The Kappa Dent

Kappas have dents on their heads that hold water. When they're on land, the water keeps them strong. Otherwise, they get so weak they can't stand up.

Stories say that kappas admire good manners. In Japan, people greet each other with a bow. To please a kappa, people are supposed to bow very low

to it. The kappa will bow very low in return.

When the kappa bows, water splashes out of the dent in its head. Then the kappa gets so weak, it can't do any harm.

Some people in Japan still believe

that kappas are real. Maybe they're bowing to one right now. Or maybe a kappa is flying around someone's garden looking for a big, juicy cucumber. And if it doesn't find one, kids better watch out!

Loch means lake in Scottish.

The Loch Ness Monster

There is a beautiful lake in Scotland called Loch Ness. For years, there have been sightings of a huge creature in the lake. People have named it Nessie.

Reports say that Nessie has a hump on her back and a long snakelike neck. Some say she's fifty feet long.

That's about the same as a Tyrannosaurus rex!

Photos and Films

Over the years, at least four thousand people claim to have seen Nessie.

One of the first sightings was in AD 565, over 1,400 years ago.

There are even a few blurry photographs and films of Nessie. Most are hard to see.

In 1934, a doctor showed pictures he claimed to have taken of Nessie. People believed the photos were real.

Years later, experts found out that the pictures were a trick. The doctor had made a tiny submarine. He fitted it with a fake sea serpent's head and took a photograph of it.

A few years ago, scientists used small submarines and underwater cameras to look for Nessie. Nothing showed up.

Later, there were sonar scans of the lake. Some of them showed that *maybe* something huge was moving in the murky waters.

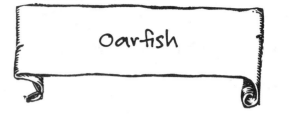

Oarfish

What sailors thought were sea serpents might have been oarfish instead.

Oarfish live in deep waters. They are the longest bony fish in the world. Their fins look like oars. Because oarfish can live 3,000 feet down in the ocean, they are rarely seen. They eat plankton, not people.

In 2013, two oarfish washed up dead on a California beach. One was twelve feet long; the other was eighteen feet long. These oarfish were actually fairly small. Some can be over fifty-six feet long and weigh up to 600 pounds!

4

Unicorns and Mermaids

Tales about mermaids and unicorns have enchanted people for thousands of years.

One of the most loved children's stories is "The Little Mermaid," written by Hans Christian Andersen in 1837.

Unicorns and mermaids are among the most popular mythical creatures. They've been in movies and on television. Pictures of mermaids and unicorns decorate T-shirts, signs, and logos. There are unicorn and mermaid stuffed animals, toys, and books.

Unicorns

Unicorn tales began more than 4,000 years ago. They got their start in the Indus Valley, in what is now part of Pakistan and India.

Over the years, unicorn stories spread to ancient Greece, Rome, and many other countries.

Pliny the Elder wrote that unicorns lived in the Indus Valley. He described them as having the head of a horse, feet like an elephant, and a three-foot-long black horn sticking out from their forehead. He claimed that their sound was like a deep bellow.

Middle Ages

In the Middle Ages, people imagined a different unicorn. A medieval unicorn

62

is like a small white horse with a spiral ivory horn growing from its forehead. Its tail looked like a lion's or a horse's. Many pictures showed unicorns with a goat's beard under their chins.

They were also often described as having the body of a goat.

To Catch a Unicorn

Unicorns are supposed to be very hard to catch. The only way to capture one is to send a young, unmarried girl into the forest. A unicorn will come out to greet her and put its head in her lap. As the girl strokes it, the unicorn will fall into a deep sleep. Hunters

Not fair to capture these good creatures!

hidden behind the trees would then rush out and capture or kill it.

Unicorn Horns Cure All

Many people wanted unicorn horns. Sailors often sold what they claimed were real unicorn horns.

To make sure a horn wasn't a fake, people were supposed to put a spider inside of it. If the spider burst, the horn was real. Maybe Queen Elizabeth should have tried this with the horn the explorer gave her. That spider would have lived!

In the 1600s, doctors used powdered "unicorn" horns as medicine. They believed that the powder protected people from poison and helped them get well.

There was a recipe for a unicorn powder that was supposed to cure almost every disease there was!

The Vikings were big sellers of narwhal horns.

What were sold as unicorn horns were actually narwhal tusks. Real unicorn horns have never existed.

Mix six grains each of: hart's horn (the horn of a red deer), pearls, ivory, and unicorn horn.
Beat them into a fine powder.

Mermaids

Mermaid tales first came from Syria over 3,000 years ago. Sailors spread these stories when they sailed to ports in the Near East, Asia, Africa, and Europe. After people heard the stories, they guessed that mermaids might live in their own rivers, lakes, and oceans.

Males are called mermen.

Mermaids are creatures of the sea. They have an upper body like a woman's. The rest of their body is a fish's tail. In stories around the world, mermaids have combs, mirrors, and long hair.

Mermaids are powerful creatures. At times, they are helpful and bring good luck. Other times, they are so cruel that they sink ships and drown sailors.

Haitian mermaid Lasirèn

Christopher Columbus's Mermaids

Christopher Columbus had heard that mermaids were beautiful. He was in for a big surprise. In 1493, when his ship was near Haiti, Columbus thought he saw three mermaids floating in the waves.

But Columbus was really upset. The mermaids had faces like a man's! They were not beautiful at all.

What Columbus most likely saw were manatees. While they are wonderful animals, they're really not much like beautiful mermaids.

This manatee lives in the sea near Haiti.

The Mermaid of Zennor

In the village of Zennor on the coast of Cornwall, an ancient stone chair sits next to a church.

The chair honors the memory of a beautiful mermaid. She was Morveren, the daughter of the king of the ocean.

Stories say that she came to Zennor long ago when a young man named Mathew Trewella began singing in the church each evening.

When Morveren heard his wonderful voice, she crept out of the sea to listen. She fell in love with Mathew's singing, and with Mathew as well.

Every night Morveren dressed in a beautiful gown made of pearls and coral to hide her body. Then she went to the village and sat by the church to hear Mathew.

One night Morveren sighed sadly. Mathew heard her. He rushed out to find the lovely creature.

Mathew followed the mermaid as she hurried down to the sea. Together, Mathew and Morveren slowly sank beneath the waves in each other's arms. No one ever saw either of them again.

The Feejee Mermaid

In the 1840s, P. T. Barnum owned a famous museum in New York City. Barnum had lots of strange exhibits. People flocked in to see things like a flea circus, stuffed dead animals, and wax figures.

Barnum put ads in newspapers saying he had the body of a real mermaid from the

Barnum's American Museum

Feejee mermaid

Fiji Islands. He called it the Feejee Mermaid. (This is definitely not how to spell *Fiji*!)

The Feejee Mermaid wasn't real, and Barnum knew it. People were paying money to see the dried upper body of a monkey attached to a dried fish's tail. Many got really angry. Barnum didn't care. He had just gotten richer!

5

Animals in Creation Myths

Almost all cultures have tales about how the world began. They are called creation myths and are some of the oldest stories.

Many creation stories have mythical serpents, birds, and eggs in them. They show how alike people in different places can be.

The ancient Greeks told of a goddess who became a dove and laid an egg. A huge serpent coiled around the egg to keep it

Doves were a peace symbol in Greece and many other cultures.

warm. When the egg finally hatched, the world and all its rivers, mountains, and oceans sprang into being.

Ancient Egypt

Ancient Egyptian creation myths center around a bird that looks like a heron. Before the earth began, this bird flew over the dead waters covering the earth.

The bird landed on a rock and let out a loud and mighty cry. Its voice broke the endless silence. Time began, and the whole world started to wake up.

Africa

There are West African creation myths about a goddess and a magic serpent. The serpent put the goddess, Mawu, in his mouth. Over and over again, the two circled the world together.

Whenever the serpent went to the bathroom, it left minerals behind that enriched the land.

As the serpent wound around the earth, its movements created rivers, mountains, and valleys.

This is a statue of the serpent Aido Hwedo, which circled the world with Mawu.

When the two had finished circling and the world was complete, Mawu asked the serpent to coil beneath the earth and hold it up.

Iroquois

The Iroquois (EER-oh-koy), a Native American tribe, tell a creation story about Sky Woman, who lived on a floating island in the sky. One day she fell through a hole, down to the waters below. Two birds caught her in midair and carried her on their backs to sea animals swimming in the ocean.

As Sky Woman watched, each animal dove into the water to try to bring up mud from the bottom of the sea. None of them could.

Finally Little Toad dove down and came up with a mouth full of mud. The animals spread the mud on the back of Big Turtle.

The mud grew so large that it was as big as a continent! Then Sky Woman threw dust in the air to make the stars and created the sun and the moon.

Lost Mojave Creation Songs

The Mojave (moh-HAH-vee) people have lived on the Colorado River in Arizona and California for thousands of years. They sang their creation myths rather than telling them. The songs told of their beginnings as a people and the land and river that they loved.

As time passed, many of the songs were lost. By 1972, only one Creation Song singer was left. His name was Emmett Van Fleet.

Emmett recorded all 525 songs of the Creation Song Cycle before he died. The tapes were forgotten until forty years later. Now the Mojave have an important part of their history back that once was lost.

6

Griffins and Other Mythical Beasts

How did anyone ever dream up an animal like the griffin? These strange creatures have the head, wings, and front legs of an eagle. Their bodies, tails, and back legs are like a lion's. Some stories say that griffins are as large as eight lions!

They are also supposed to be as strong as a hundred eagles. A griffin has the power and courage of a lion. It can fly as swiftly as an eagle and has its great eyesight. It's no wonder griffins were symbols of power and bravery.

Griffin Myths

Myths about griffins were common in Asia, Greece, and the rest of Europe. These strange beasts were said to live in mountains and sit on nests of gold. If anyone tried to steal their gold, the griffins would kill them and their horses, too!

Austrian coat of arms

Griffins became known as guardians and protectors. They mated for life, and if their mate died, they never took another. People had figures of griffins carved on their buildings for good luck. Griffins also appear on coats of arms and flags as a sign of strength in war.

Come on! Let's go meet some more really awesome mythical creatures!

Quetzalcoatl

The Aztec people of Mexico worshipped a mythical serpent god named Quetzalcoatl (KET-sull-koh-ah-tull). It had a snake's body and beautiful green, blue, and red feathers like those of the quetzal bird. Quetzal feathers were on the headdresses of Aztec kings and priests as a symbol of their god.

Aztecs believed that Quetzalcoatl created the universe. He was the god of the wind and the morning star.

Corn was a big part of the Aztec diet. In one story, a huge red ant led Quetzalcoatl to

a mountain covered with grains and corn.
Quetzalcoatl took the corn to the other gods.
They all agreed that it was a good food, and
people have been eating it ever since.

Kitsune

Some favorite myths in Japan are about magical foxes. The Japanese word for fox is *kitsune* (KEET-soo-nay). In myths, kitsune are known for their great wisdom. The older they get, the smarter they are.

Kitsune can live 1,000 years. By the time they are very old, it's thought that they are so wise, they know everything in the world.

When a kitsune has lived for 100 years, it grows a new tail. It can have as many as nine tails. When a kitsune gets its ninth tail, its coat turns white or gold.

Kitsune often change into beautiful women and marry men. In myths, if a man discovers his wife is a kitsune, the marriage ends. Or if dogs come snooping around, the kitsune quickly turns back into a fox and heads for the woods.

Leucrocuta

The leucrocuta of Africa is the fastest of all mythical beasts. It can outrun any animal, including a gazelle.

The leucrocuta comes from a lioness and a hyena. It has a horse's or badger's head and is the size of a donkey.

This strange animal has a mouth that stretches from ear to ear and sharp, bony gums instead of teeth. It laughs and makes other noises that sound just like humans.

Stories say that if people hear the leucrocuta calling their names and go to investigate, the leucrocuta will grind them to bits with its razor-sharp gums.

The Sphinx

Four thousand years ago, the ancient Egyptians made a huge statue of a mythical animal called a sphinx. It has the body of a lion and the head of a person. Experts think the sphinx was there to guard the tombs of Egyptian kings.

The ancient Greeks also had myths about the sphinx. In one story, a sphinx struck terror into the hearts of a Greek town called Thebes. The sphinx said that she would kill all the townspeople unless someone answered her riddle.

The riddle was: What animal has four legs in the morning, two at noon, and three in the evening? One man solved it. He said that the answer was a person.

Think about it. Babies crawl on four legs. Adults walk on two legs. And when they get old, they might need a cane, which gives them three legs.

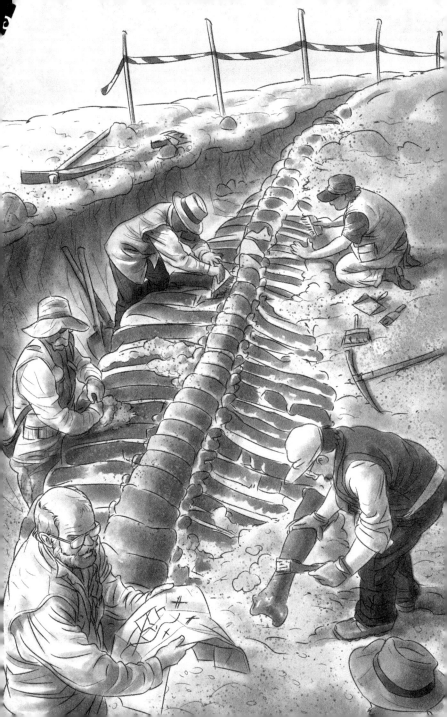

7

Mythical or Real?

How did all of these imaginary animals come into being? Many of them may be based on real animals.

Have you ever seen pictures of a giant squid? They are truly scary-looking animals.

Giant squids live so deep in the ocean that humans rarely see them. The largest ever found washed up on a beach. It was about fifty-six feet long and weighed a ton!

That's as long as a bus!

These squid have eight arms, power-ful jaws, eyes as large as basketballs, and a mouth like a parrot's sharp beak. Two long tentacles reach out to capture prey.

Sperm whales can be over fifty feet long.

Giant squid are so fearless that they can attack and kill gigantic sperm whales.

What the Sailors Saw

It's almost certain that sailors saw a giant squid instead of a kraken. It must have been a terrifying sight! And that's probably how stories of kraken got their start.

Miners Find a Griffin?

Fossils of a dinosaur called a *Protocera-tops* are often found in the Gobi Desert. Its skeleton looks a lot like a griffin. Two thousand years ago, gold miners in the

Gobi easily could have found these fossils near their gold mines. Do you remember that griffins guarded gold?

Protoceratops

The miners didn't know dinosaurs had existed. They probably imagined that the bones belonged to a fierce monster. And that monster became a griffin!

Dragons

Dragons look a lot like giant lizards. There is no scarier lizard than the Komodo dragon. These creatures are found on five islands in Indonesia. Komodos can be ten feet long and weigh 300 pounds.

Komodo dragons have toxins in their saliva. Its bite is usually deadly to people and other animals.

Komodos are meat-eaters. They'll eat water buffalo, pigs, and you! And they look a lot like the way we picture dragons.

Chinese Dragons

The idea for Chinese dragons may also have come from dinosaur bones. Over a thousand years ago, a Chinese writer described seeing the bones of a dragon. We now know they were the fossil remains of a dinosaur called a *Stegosaurus*.

China has more dinosaur fossils than any other country. Even today some Chinese people find dinosaur bones that they believe are dragon bones. They grind them up to use in medicines.

99

The woolly rhinoceros is extinct.

Unicorns or Rhinos?

Some think that unicorn stories began with an Ice Age woolly rhinoceros called an *Elasmotherium.*

It had one horn and moved like a horse. Ice Age humans knew about woolly rhinos. They hunted them, and there are even cave paintings of them.

Experts wonder if the idea for unicorns could have sprung from ancient tales of this extinct animal.

Marco Polo was a great explorer in the thirteenth century. He wrote a lot about his travels. Marco Polo thought he saw a real unicorn. He described it as being as big as an elephant. From his description, it's fairly certain that Marco Polo actually saw a Javan rhino.

Javan rhinoceros

Without the Facts

People long ago were just as smart as we are today. But they didn't have good information. They had ideas, but they didn't have facts. They couldn't possibly know much about fossils and dinosaurs. Today we know more than ever before. Pliny the Elder would be amazed at all we've learned.

Digging Up Myths

Sometimes legends grow out of true events. Remember the story of the red and white dragons? In 1945, a team of archaeologists in Wales began to look for the ruins of the real King Vortigern's castle. The site was on a mountain in a place called Dinas Emrys. In tales of Merlin's boyhood, Emrys is his last name.

Much to their surprise, the team uncovered a pond. In the story, the dragons were supposed to be sleeping in a lake. There were also ruins of a fort dating back a thousand years, to Vortigern's time.

And most exciting of all, they discovered that the fort had been destroyed and rebuilt several different times! The only thing the archaeologists didn't uncover were sleeping dragons.

Almost nothing remains of the famous fort in Wales where the dragons were said to have fought.

8

Mythical Creatures Today

Even today we create new myths. We have mythical creatures on TV, in the movies, and in books. The difference is that we know most of them are only make-believe. But there are some modern myths that just won't die.

One modern mythical animal is *Bigfoot*, or *Sasquatch*. Bigfoot is said to live in Asia and in the western United States.

Bigfoot is covered in reddish brown

fur and can stand eight feet tall. Bigfoot hunters keep looking for traces of this hairy creature, which is said to walk on two legs.

One man said he was captured by a Bigfoot family and escaped after six days.

He claimed he gave them chewing tobacco that made them so sick he was able to get away.

In 1967, two men said they made a film of a female Bigfoot striding through the forest. Some people thought that it was a person dressed in a gorilla costume. Others said they couldn't tell exactly what it was. Stories about Bigfoot sightings still make the news.

Yeti

In the Himalayan Mountains, some people think an animal much like Bigfoot is roaming around. People have named it the yeti, or the Abominable Snowman.

Yeti is a Tibetan word meaning rock bear.

People claim to have seen a hairy creature walking on two legs. There have also been reports of huge footprints in the snow. In 1951, one was found on Mount Everest in the Himalayas.

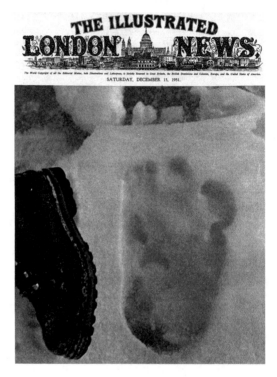

In 1953, Sir Edmund Hillary, a famous mountain climber, searched for the yeti.

When he didn't see any signs of a yeti, he decided that the print was really made by a Himalayan brown bear.

Sir Edmund Hillary and his guide, Tenzing Norgay, were the first people to climb to the top of Mount Everest.

Why?

Why do we still tell stories about imaginary creatures? Something about them fascinates us. These stories feed our imaginations and make our lives richer.

Being a little scared is sometimes fun, especially if there's really nothing to be scared of. If you think a monster might be under your bed, don't worry! There is nothing under your bed or in your closet either.

So settle down and read a good book before you fall asleep. One about dragons, unicorns, mermaids, or other mythical creatures would be perfect.

Doing More Research

There's a lot more you can learn about dragons and mythical creatures. The fun of research is seeing how many different sources you can explore.

Books

Most libraries and bookstores have books about mythical animals.

Here are some things to remember when you're using books for research:

1. You don't have to read the whole book. Check the table of contents and the index to find the topics you're interested in.

2. Write down the name of the book.

When you take notes, make sure you write down the name of the book in your notebook so you can find it again.

3. Never copy exactly from a book.

When you learn something new from a book, put it in your own words.

4. Make sure the book is <u>nonfiction</u>.

Some books tell make-believe stories about mythical creatures. Make-believe stories are called *fiction*. They're fun to read, but not good for research.

Research books have facts and tell true stories. They are called *nonfiction*. A librarian or teacher can help you make sure the books you use for research are nonfiction.

Here are some good nonfiction books about mythical creatures:

- *Bestiary: An Illuminated Alphabet of Medieval Beasts* by Jonathan Hunt
- *Children's Book of Mythical Beasts and Magical Monsters* by DK Publishing
- *A Field Guide to Griffins, Unicorns, and Other Mythical Beasts* by A. J. Sautter
- *Monsterology: The Complete Book of Monstrous Beasts* by Dr. Ernest Drake
- *Mythical Monsters: The Scariest Creatures from Legends, Books, and Movies* by Chris McNab

Museums

Many museums can help you learn more about dragons and mythical animals.

When you go to a museum:

1. Be sure to take your notebook!
Write down anything that catches your interest. Draw pictures, too!

2. Ask questions.
There are almost always people at museums who can help you find what you're looking for.

3. Check the calendar.
Many museums have special events and activities just for kids!

Here are some museums with medieval and Asian exhibits:

- Art Institute of Chicago
- Arthur M. Sackler Museum (Cambridge, Massachusetts)
- Asian Art Museum of San Francisco
- The Cloisters (New York)
- Metropolitan Museum of Art (New York)
- Nelson-Atkins Museum of Art (Kansas City, Missouri)

The Internet

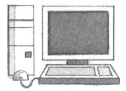

Many websites have lots of facts about mythical animals. Some also have games and activities that can help make learning about them even more fun.

Ask your teacher or your parents to help you find more websites like these:

- amnh.org/exhibitions/mythic-creatures
- animalplanet.com/tv-shows/monster -week/mythical-animals-that-turned-out -to-be-real
- dragonsforkids.co.uk/dragon-facts
- history.com/news/history-lists /6-mythical-monsters
- kidzsearch.com/wiki/Unicorn
- ngkids.co.uk/history/Greek-Myths
- tor.com/2012/08/13/sea-monsters-a-z

Good luck!

Bibliography

Allan, Tony. *The Mythic Bestiary: The Illustrated Guide to the World's Most Fantastical Creatures*. London: Duncan Baird, 2008.

Bates, Roy. *Chinese Dragons* (Images of Asia). New York: Oxford University Press, 2002.

Eggleton, Bob. *The Book of Sea Monsters*. New York: Overlook Press, 1998.

Huber, Richard. *Treasury of Fantastic and Mythological Creatures*. Mineola: Dover Publications, 1981.

Nigg, Joe. *The Book of Dragons & Other Mythical Beasts*. London: Quantum, 2006.

Van Duzer, Chet. *Sea Monsters on Medieval and Renaissance Maps*. London: British Library Publishing, 2014.

Index

Photographs courtesy of:

Have you read the adventure that matches
up with this book?

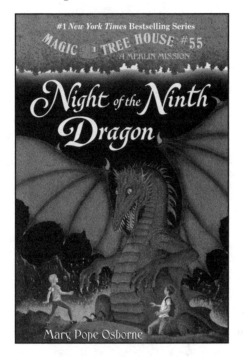

Don't miss Magic Tree House® #55:
Night of the Ninth Dragon!
Jack and Annie return to Camelot in a
thrilling adventure steeped in history!

If you liked Magic Tree House® Super Edition #1: *World at War, 1944* (formerly *Danger in the Darkest Hour*), you'll love finding out the facts behind the fiction in

Magic Tree House®
Fact Tracker
World War II

A nonfiction companion to
Magic Tree House® Super Edition #1:

World at War, 1944

It's Jack and Annie's very own guide
to World War II.

Coming in January 2017

BRING MAGIC TREE HOUSE TO YOUR SCHOOL!

Magic Tree House musicals now available for performance by young people!

Ask your teacher or director to contact Music Theatre International for more information:
BroadwayJr.com
Licensing@MTIshows.com
(212) 541-4684

MAGIC TREE HOUSE COLLECTION
DINOSAURS BEFORE DARK KIDS

MAGIC TREE HOUSE COLLECTION
The **Knight at Dawn** KIDS

ATTENTION, TEACHERS!

Mary Pope Osborne's
Classroom Adventures Program

The Magic Tree House **CLASSROOM ADVENTURES PROGRAM** is a free, comprehensive set of online educational resources for teachers developed by Mary Pope Osborne as a gift to teachers, to thank them for their enthusiastic support of the series. Educators can learn more at MTHClassroomAdventures.org.

MAGIC TREE HOUSE